# FINE ARTS AND CRAFTS

# FINE ARTS AND CRAFTS

MURIEL MILLER BRANCH

*African-American Arts*

TWENTY-FIRST CENTURY BOOKS
BROOKFIELD, CONNECTICUT

Twenty-First Century Books
A Division of The Millbrook Press
2 Old New Milford Road
Brookfield, Connecticut 06804

Library of Congress Cataloging-in-Publication Data
Branch, Muriel Miller.
Fine arts and crafts / Muriel Miller Branch.
p. cm. — (African-American arts)
Includes bibliographical references and index.
ISBN 0-7613-1868-2 (lib. bdg.)
1. African American art. 2. African American folk art. 3. Art, American. I. Title. II. Series.
N6538.N5 B73 2001
704.03'96073—dc21   2001027166

Cover photographs courtesy of Hampton University Museum, Hampton, Virginia (*The Banjo Lesson* by Henry Ossawa Tanner); Fine Arts Museums of San Francisco, Lent by the Federal Art Project, X1993.1 (*Standing Woman*, 1934 by Sargent Claude Johnson); Virginia Museum of Fine Arts, Richmond. Gift of Dr. and Mrs. Jeffrey Hammer. Photo by Katherine Wetzel. © Virginia Museum of Fine Arts (Egungun Mask)

Photographs courtesy of © Virginia Museum of Fine Arts, Richmond: pp. 8 (The Adolph D. and Wilkins C. Williams Fund, photo: Katherine Wetzel), 11 (Gift of Dr. and Mrs. Jeffrey Hammer, photo: Katherine Wetzel), 13 (inset: The Adolph D. and Wilkins C. Williams Fund, photo: Katherine Wetzel), 19 (from *African Art/Virginia Museum of Fine Arts* by Richard Woodward); © John Pemberton III: p. 10; © Pascal James Imperato: p. 13; National Museum of American History, Smithsonian Institution: p. 20; the Collections of the South Carolina Historical Society: p. 24; Library of Congress: pp. 29, 82; Bowdoin College Museum of Art, Brunswick, Maine, Museum Purchase, George Otis Hamlin Fund: p. 31; Howard University Gallery of Art, Washington, D.C.: pp. 33, 37; Smithsonian American Art Museum: pp. 35 (# 1983.95.62 Gift of G. William Miller), 57 (# 1994.17 Gift of the Historical Society of Forest Park, Illinois), 66 (#1967.57.28 Gift of the Harmon Foundation), 67 (1981.1441 Gift of Elizabeth Gibbons-Hanson), 69 (#1967.59.1055 Gift of the Harmon Foundation), 73 (#1981.136.5A Gift of Chuck and Jan Rosenak); Wadsworth Atheneum, Hartford. The Ella Gallup Sumner and Mary Catlin Sumner Collection Fund: p. 36; Hampton University Museum, Hampton, Virginia: p. 39; National Archives: pp. 43 (#200S HN MOT 8), 45 (#200S HN WA 13); © Jeff Donaldson: p. 46; © Robert A. Sengstacke: p. 47; The Phillips Collection, Washington, D.C.: p. 49; © Elizabeth Catlett/Licensed by VAGA, New York, NY: p. 50; © Samella Lewis/Licensed by VAGA, New York, NY: p. 51; Smithsonian American Art Museum, Washington, D.C./Art Resource, NY: p. 53; Virginia Historical Society, Richmond, Virginia: p. 55; Arts & Artifacts Division, Schomburg Center for Research in Black Culture, Astor, Lenox and Tilden Foundations, The New York Public Library: pp. 58, 61, 62, 84; Fine Arts Museums of San Francisco, Lent by the Federal Arts Project, X1993.1: p. 59; Fisk University: pp. 71, 85; The Pennsylvania Academy of the Fine Arts, Philadelphia. John Lambert Fund, 1943.11: p. 72; the Collection of Ron and June Shelp: p. 74; © 1997 Donna Van Der Zee: p. 79; Hampton University Archives: p. 86; Kathy Rinehart/Addison Gallery of Art: p. 88

# CONTENTS

## Acknowledgments

I am grateful for the willing assistance of staff members at The Library of Virginia, the Virginia Museum of Fine Arts, especially Dr. Suzanne H. Truman and Rebecca Do Byns; The Arts and Humanities Center of Richmond Public Schools; Central Library, Chesterfield Public Library; The Smithsonian Institution, Museum of American Art; Winterthur Museum; and the Hampton University Museum. I owe a personal debt to authors Brent Ashabranner and Mary Lyons for previous works on the topic; artist Dennis R. Winston for checking my art facts; friend Naana Biney-Amissah for sharing her cultural traditions; my resident readers and critics, Willis L. Branch and Missouri W. Miller, for their critical listening ears; and my friend and technology guru, Veronica A. Davis, for reformatting the manuscript in its early stages.

# INTRODUCTION

When you are introduced to someone, you shake his or her hand, and say, "It's nice to meet you." Sometimes the sincerity of her handshake or smile causes you to think, Gee, I like this person. If there is that immediate bond, you'll probably exchange phone numbers or e-mail addresses, or arrange to meet again. Each time you talk, you will learn more about each other.

The same is true with *Fine Arts and Crafts*. You cannot possibly learn everything you'd like to know about the contributions of three centuries of African-American artists in ninety-six pages. So, what this book does is serve as that first handshake, connecting you to the lives of a few courageous and talented African-American artists. Hopefully, you will be curious enough about them to want to know more. To answer any lingering questions, I invite you to spend time reading about black artists in the books listed in the bibliography; visiting one or all of the six historically black colleges or the numerous museums where their works are on exhibit; and researching their lives and careers online.

*Ifa diviner's box (wood). Late nineteenth to early*
*twentieth century. Nigeria, Republic of Benin. Virginia Museum*
*of Fine Arts, Richmond. The Adolph D. and Wilkins C. Williams Fund.*

# ONE

# CROSSING THE ATLANTIC

## AFRICAN ART
## SURVIVES IN AMERICA

Art was as tightly woven into African cultures as the threads of an Ashanti kente robe. Just as it's nearly impossible to distinguish where each thread in a robe intersects, it's equally difficult to separate art from African cultural and religious beliefs and rituals. Explains renowned author, collector, and art historian Dr. Regenia A. Perry, "Traditional West Africans [the relatives of most Americans who descended from slaves] are intensely spiritual, and religion, art and music are important and inseparable entities of that universe."

Like other ancient religions, African traditional religion showed the way people thought about themselves in relation to the universe, God, spirits, nature, human life, and the hereafter. Rituals were used as an outward demonstration of those beliefs. Because art was almost always created in connection with those religious rituals and ceremonies, it also helped to interpret the beliefs of the people. From birth to death, art and religion were intersecting threads of African life.

In the Yoruba culture of Nigeria, the Ifa, or diviner, was second in rank only to the chief or king. Trained as a priest, the Ifa had the power to interpret the ways of the gods. People came to him to learn the future. The Ifa stored his sacred tools in a decorative bag or an intricately carved wooden divination box with four or five separate compartments. The box was carved with important symbols such as "human characters, spirits, and rituals," writes Richard B. Woodward, curator of African Art at the Virginia Museum of Fine Arts in Richmond, Virginia. The relief, or raised carvings, on the lid often represented the constant battle between two spirits: Eshu, a trickster who caused chaos, and Orunmila, the god of wisdom who restored order.

*Yoruba king wearing a beaded crown (cloth, beads, threads). 1971. Nigeria.*

*Egungun mask (cloth, wood, metal). Twentieth century. Nigeria, Republic of Benin. Virginia Museum of Fine Arts, Richmond. Gift of Dr. and Mrs. Jeffrey Hammer.*

Queen mothers adorned their necks and ears with beautifully crafted gold and copper jewelry at village festivals, to show their wealth and status in the community. When "holding court," making decisions, or settling disputes, a Yoruba king (*oba*) donned a crown decorated with thousands of miniature beads. The crown, which came down over the king's face, was made to protect his "inner head." The design of the mask was important, for Yoruba people believed the king's inner head united with the heads of kings who had reigned before him.

A mask represented the most visible communal art because it was "the focal point of initiation rites, funerals, dances, authority symbols, protection symbols, and spiritual embodiments among the African people," report the authors of African-Americans in the Visual Arts: A Historical Perspective, a

Web site devoted to African-American art. Accompanied by the vigorous rhythm of drums, art came alive with movement as dancers in spectacular *Egungun* masks performed to honor the dead. These masked dancers also wore brilliantly colored costumes composed of hundreds of strips of cloth attached to a board. As they whirled and twirled, the colorful strips billowed out to call up the ancestral spirits to the world of the living.

Art also marked the passage of time, and played a vital role in the ceremonies and rituals celebrating births, marriages, harvests, and deaths. An example of one of those rituals was the "naming" and "outdooring" ceremony practiced by the Fante culture (the Akan peoples of Ghana, West Africa).

The outdooring and naming ceremony was a social event that introduced and welcomed a newborn into the family. The naming ceremony meant a lot to the Fante, because they believed that the child's character was influenced by the character of the person whose name he or she was given. "The 'naming' and 'outdooring' ceremony was really important in my culture," said Ghanaian-American Naana Biney-Amissah. "It was customary to wait until the eighth day to name and outdoor the baby, because we believed that the first seven days she was just visiting the family. During the ceremony, a tiny gold ring was placed on the infant's finger by his or her father to symbolize the continuation of life," she explained.

On the day of his stages of life ceremony, a Yoruba boy received the gift of a splendidly carved drum to play during his initiation to manhood. To insure a young Akan (Ghanaian) bride the ability to bear children, a priest consecrated and presented her with an *Akuaba*, or fertility doll. Believed to have spiritual powers to promote childbearing, the doll was tucked inside the young woman's waistcloth, carried on her back, and treated like a real baby until she had a child of her own.

Exquisitely carved ivory horns trumpeted the arrival of chiefs and queen mothers. A wooden headrest provided the "pillow" for a good night's sleep or kept an elaborate hairstyle in place.

According to art historians, Africans used art to interact with or control their environment. Among the Bambara, or Bamana, people in Western Sudan (Mali), a dance headdress in the form of an antelope represented *Chi*

*Chi Wara (Tyi Wara) dancers. Segou Region, Mali. Inset: Chi Wara headdress (wood). Nineteenth to twentieth century. Mali. Virginia Museum of Fine Arts, Richmond. The Adolph D. and Wilkins C. Williams Fund.*

*Wara*, the spirit that introduced agriculture to the region. Chi Wara was invited back to the farming villages for the annual planting festivals. By invoking his presence in a ceremony that celebrated the antelope's early role in teaching the people to farm, it was believed that the village of the Bambara would be assured a successful farming season. Two headdresses were created, one male and one female. Young men of the *flankuru*, or cooperating groups of farmers, danced in these headdresses from sunup to sundown, imitating the planting movements, while other villagers sang songs praising the spirit of Chi Wara.

This was the world of art West Africans lived in for centuries before being brutally cut off from their traditions by the crime of slavery. And this was the world that the first few generations of enslaved Africans remembered. To them, art had meaning and purpose. Art was shared. As one art historian wrote, "African art is created not so much to express the artist's personality as to serve the community."

## AFRICAN ART IN AMERICA

This appreciation of art in all its forms survived even the perilous journey across the Atlantic. Drums and music were probably the earliest and most widespread ways of communicating among enslaved Africans in the Americas. Many stories are told about how the "talking drums," used in Africa to send messages between villages, were adapted in colonial America to serve a very similar purpose. By the early 1800s, the drum was such a powerful form of communication among enslaved Africans that slaveholders outlawed its use.

Art was also valuable in helping enslaved Africans from different cultures understand each other. Regardless of language differences, there were certain symbols in art and certain uses of art objects that were as universal as the shared musical traditions. Since Africans in America viewed art as part of their spiritual heritage, the use of religious symbols gained importance during the eighteenth and nineteenth centuries. Because bondsmen were not allowed by their owners to practice traditional African religions, they often cleverly combined their religious beliefs with Christian rituals.

"Animals, birds, serpents and other reptiles have always figured prominently in traditional West African religions and mythology," writes Dr. Regenia A. Perry. So it's natural that these familiar "motifs" showed up on numerous carved items in America. The most noted examples are the wooden walking canes carved by a slave named **Henry Gudgell**. One of his works, *Carved cane with figured relief*, about 1867, resembles a bronze walking stick found in Nigeria. Read from top to bottom, the relief images on both canes tell the story of a serpent ready to attack. These familiar symbols also showed up in quilts and other crafts created by enslaved Africans.

Some of these handicrafts were created for the slaves' own use. Others were produced for slave masters, either for their households or for sale. For as whites in colonial America and Europe developed an appetite for handicrafts and other goods, they began to rely on slaves and free Africans as a source of cheap or free labor to produce them.

African artists used their skills, even in creating the most ordinary objects such as quilts, walking canes, and jugs, to pass on their culture. They painted, sculpted, carved, and forged their way into the artistic history of America.

# TWO

# HOMEMADE
## ARTS AND CRAFTS

Today, our idea of a mechanic is a man or woman who works on automobiles or other machinery. As early as the mid-seventeenth century, the terms mechanic, artisan, tradesman, and craftsman were used interchangeably to refer to the highly skilled men and women who made things by hand. These skilled workers, both black and white, free and slave, kept the wheels of the northern and southern economies rolling.

In the seventeenth and early eighteenth centuries, white indentured servants (people who served a master for a specified period of time) provided much of the needed skilled labor. But as colonists began to diversify, or branch out, into producing other products, the need for more skilled laborers became critical. Slave labor provided the solution to the problem; it was plentiful and it was free. The practice of apprenticing Africans to white master craftsmen became a lucrative business for slave owners, because they made more money hiring out their slaves than having them work in the fields. By the mid-1800s thousands of slaves were working in every trade imaginable.

In the northern colonies, slaves and free blacks worked alongside their masters and mentors as coopers (barrel and keg makers), silversmiths and engravers (jewelers), and shipwrights (shipbuilders) in the large northern seaports of Massachusetts and New York. Southern slaves tanned leather and made shoes, spun and wove cloth in loom houses, built huge mansions, and handcrafted most of the iron tools needed in farming.

## AFRICAN SKILLS

Many Africans brought their skills from their homelands. Africans were skilled at, among many things, forging or shaping farm tools; making weights from copper, bronze, or brass to measure gold dust; weaving baskets; making textiles; and building houses. After all, they helped build the city of Timbuktu, one of the richest cultural and commercial centers of ancient Africa.

Yet Africans, regardless of their level of skill, had to be retrained by white craftsmen to do things the American way. First, Africans were not accustomed to mass production. They created art from the *kra*, or soul, and for the benefit of the community. Second, they were expected to imitate European style rather than follow the very controlled styles of their native lands. In addition, retraining was necessary because skilled enslaved craftsmen, especially in the ironworks and carpentry trades, threatened white artisans, who feared the competition. In fact, laws were passed in the South to prohibit the hiring of slave artisans over white craftsmen. White craftsmen wanted to establish that Africans were inferior and incapable of doing skilled work.

And, finally, retraining may have been a deliberate attempt to wipe out any use of African symbols or meanings that might aid slave artisans in communicating with other slaves. As a result, slave-made artifacts were often destroyed or condemned as pagan or sinful. The only acceptable slave work was created under the watchful eyes of white men, who often took credit for it. For this reason, the proof that certain articles were made by individual slave craftsmen may be forever buried with their bones. Anonymity is the legacy of the slave artisan—their identities virtually erased by the use of words such as "parcel" or "lot" to identify them [slaves] in newspaper advertisements, auction broadsides, and court records.

Despite the restrictions and the labels of inferiority placed on the slave artisan, "highly patterned raffia basketry; religious voodoo objects such as the so-called slave mask; and carved wooden grave markers bear witness to the fact that certain African forms made their way into American society during the period," writes author and art collector David Driskell.

According to noted artist and art historian Samella Lewis, two types of slave crafts survived from the colonial period: articles designed for the slaves' personal use (quilts, pottery, shell beads, dolls, bone carvings, staffs, baskets, gravestones) and articles made for whites' public or professional use.

## QUILTS

Slave seamstresses stitched museum-quality quilts for their mistresses, while using the leftover scraps to make patchwork, strip, crazy, and Bible quilts for their own families. From tiny pieces of worn-out material, these women created quilts that not only kept the family warm but also preserved the textile traditions of their African ancestors.

African influences are easily seen in the recurring themes and symbols appearing on slave quilts, such as the diamond shape, large bold colors and patterns, and zigzag lines. The diamond was a Kongo symbol that represented the four stages of life as seen in the phases of the sun: dawn (birth), noon (maturity), sunset (death), and midnight (realm of the ancestors). The zigzag patterns can be traced back to the African traditional belief that evil travels in a straight line. The use of strong bold patterns and colors was a carryover from West African weaving traditions that date back to ancient times. Other traditions included a preference for alternate rather than repeating patterns and the use of protective charms to safeguard the user from evil spirits.

The technique of appliqué is found in the royal tapestries of Dahomey in what is today the Republic of Benin. Made by men for the royal family, these works of art hung in palace halls to tell the story of victories in battle as well as the history of the royal family. The appliqué technique is a multistep process that involves cutting out lots of symbols from brightly colored cloth and stitching them onto a plain background.

Before the invention of the sewing machine, enslaved women in the United States sewed appliquéd quilts by hand. Perhaps the most noted quilt artist was **Harriet Powers**, a former slave. Embellished with religious and historical symbols, her appliquéd quilts told of biblical and celestial events.

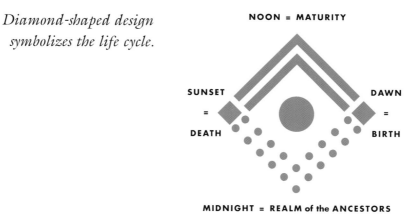

*Diamond-shaped design symbolizes the life cycle.*

NOON = MATURITY

SUNSET = DEATH

DAWN

BIRTH

MIDNIGHT = REALM of the ANCESTORS

Other enslaved women stitched secret symbols in quilt patterns to tell family histories or to lead a fellow slave to freedom. Some historians have called these quilts "scrapbooks" because they kept a record of family histories. The creator of a quilt titled *Black Family Album* (1854) used the technique of appliqué to literally paste her family album onto a lasting fabric.

## CLOTHING

**Elizabeth Hobbs Keckley** (1818–1907) was among the legions of enslaved seamstresses whose deft hands were put to use designing and making fashionable dresses for their mistresses. Keckley was born into slavery in Dinwiddie Court House, Virginia. Trained by her mother on the Burwell plantation there, Keckley showed an early talent for sewing. "Mrs. Burwell [was] a hard task-master, and as my mother had so much work to do in making clothes, etc., I determined to render her all the assistance in my power. . . ." explained Keckley in her autobiography, *Behind the Scenes: Thirty Years as a Slave and Four Years at the White House.*

At fourteen she was sent to live with Reverend Robert Burwell, her master's son, a minister who lived in Hillsboro, North Carolina. According to her memoirs, her darkest days as a slave were spent in Hillsboro, where she was repeat-

Bible Quilt *(pieced and appliquéd cotton)* by Harriet Powers. About 1886.
*National Museum of American History, Washington, D.C.*

edly whipped to "subdue her stubborn pride." The final humiliation came when she was raped by a man she never named and bore a "near white son."

Several years later, Keckley went to work for Anne, another member of the Burwell family. Anne and her husband moved to Missouri and took Keckley, her son, and her mother with them. There, Keckley became a seamstress, sewing for both her mistress and other prominent white women in the area.

By 1855, Keckley was able to purchase freedom for herself and her son through loans made her by her lady patrons. "The twelve hundred dollars was raised, and at last my son and I were free. Free, free! What a glorious ring to the word. Free! The bitter hard struggle was over. Free!" she exclaimed.

Subsequently, Keckley left St. Louis. Eventually she settled in Washington, D.C., where she found employment as the dressmaker for such dignitaries as Varina Howell Davis, the wife of the Confederate president, Jefferson Davis. During this period, Keckley founded the First Black Contraband Relief Association, an organization formed to aid slaves in Washington, D.C., who had escaped to Union territory.

In 1861, Mary Todd Lincoln, the wife of President Abraham Lincoln, hired Elizabeth Keckley as her personal dressmaker. Later, Keckley and Mary Todd Lincoln had a falling out over Keckley's memoirs, *Behind the Scenes*, in which she recounted her life in the Lincoln White House and described the president's wife as an overly ambitious, jealous, acid-tongued spendthrift. In writing so candidly about her former employer, Keckley may have unwittingly stepped over the line, especially since she revealed personal conversations between herself and the first lady. Their differences were never resolved, and, as a result, Keckley's customers no longer patronized her. Furthermore, when *Behind the Scenes* was published, Mrs. Lincoln's eldest son, Robert, was so angry that he halted publication of future editions. Keckley died penniless in the Home for Destitute Women and Children in Washington, D.C.

## POTTERY

The works of a slave potter named **Dave [David Drake]** shed light on the dim life of slave potters. Dave (1800?–1870?) worked for forty years in a little community called Edgefield, South Carolina, creating huge alkaline-glazed vessels that ranged in color from oatmeal beige to olive green. Some vessels measured as high as 27 inches (68 centimeters) and as round as the trunk of a mature oak tree. So immense were Dave's storage jars that, for effect, collectors Mary and Jimmy Smith of Augusta, Georgia, had a photograph taken of their little girl inside one of them.

The author of *"I made this jar . . . Dave": The Life and Works of the Enslaved African-American Potter, Dave* explained how Dave produced such massive pots. "Dave made these huge pots by joining separately made sec-

*Dave's pottery. 1840. Collection of the Charleston Museum, South Carolina.*

tions. The base was turned on the [potter's] wheel, the upper sections were then applied to the base in coils or turned separately, joined and adhered by smoothing the clay together," she wrote.

Dave inscribed poems and sayings on his pots that give a slave's-eye glimpse of life in the nineteenth century. For instance, we learn from at least one of Dave's couplets—"Dave belongs to Mr. Miles/wher the oven bakes & the pot biles, 31st July 1840"—that his skill as a potter did not insulate him from being sold and traded. Miles was his second owner. We also discover from his inscription on an 1857 storage jar that he longed to be with his family, "I wonder where is all my relations: Friendship to all—and every nation." Dave's musings on clay clearly show that he was a poet, a philosopher, and a highly skilled artisan.

It is remarkable that so many of Dave's works survived more than 150 years. Some were uncovered as late as 1991. It's even more incredible that he was bold enough to sign his name on each vessel, defying the law prohibiting slaves from reading and writing, and that he also gave free rein to his poetic ability by personalizing each piece of pottery with a witty inscription.

In a wonderful exhibit put together by the McKissick Museum in Columbia, South Carolina, twenty-five of Dave's massive pots have toured the country. According to the description of the exhibit, these works "celebrate the life of this extraordinary potter and poet who, despite the shackles of slavery, found great personal expression in his work." The traveling exhibition of Dave's works "has generated interest that has pushed previously undiscovered pieces into view," explained guest curator Jill Koverman. "They still turn up in barns; they turn up in people's pantries," she added.

Another example of slave-made pottery was uncovered a few years ago at Ibo Landing on St. Simons Island, Georgia—the famous site where eighteen men of the Ibo tribe of Nigeria committed suicide. Rather than live their lives in slavery, these African men drowned themselves in Dunbar Creek. Mrs. Robert J. Forbes, the present owner of both the property and the jug, explained that she unearthed this piece of pottery when she and her husband were clearing the land to build their home. At the time, she didn't know the value of the greenish, alkaline-coated pitcher, but kept it because it was "in such good shape."

*Akaline-coated pottery found at Ibo Landing, St. Simons Island, Georgia. Private collection.*

*Slave-made wrought-iron gate. The Collections of the South Carolina Historical Society.*

"A couple years back I showed this jug to a Nigerian visitor, and he was so surprised to see how much it looked like the pottery made in his country," Mrs. Forbes explained.

## METALWORK AND ENGRAVING

The intricate colonial iron- and metalwork on eighteenth-century mansions, churches, and public buildings was created almost entirely by black blacksmiths. The workmanship of these anonymous "smithies" was so graceful that it may well have been created to honor Ogun, the Nigerian god of iron and forging. In the Yoruba culture, Ogun is the god of all the skilled men who use metal tools: the blacksmith, the goldsmith, the butcher, the hunters and soldiers. James Newton, coeditor of *The Other Slaves*, states, "Ornamental ironwork and delicate patterns beaten out over a forge were among the most artistic creations of black craftsmen during the early days of slavery." The decorative wrought-iron grills, balconies, hinges, and gates still visible in Charleston, South Carolina, New Orleans, Louisiana, and Mobile, Alabama, are monuments to the skill of these unnamed black men.

According to numerous antebellum newspapers, skillful blacks also engraved fine designs on silver, gold, and wood in the shops of their masters. The *Maryland Gazette,* November 2, 1774, listed the sale of an unnamed slave who was skilled at "raising and making impressions in gold, silver and copper, brass, etcetera, and likewise making small cuts of all kinds, woodcuts, arms and figures on plates in the neatest manner."

Slaves also found outlets for self-expression in the handicrafts they made for their personal use, such as the coiled baskets made by Gullah weavers. The Gullah people are descendants of West Africans from Angola, Sierra Leone, Ghana, and Nigeria who were brought to the Sea Islands off the coast of South Carolina and Georgia to work on large indigo, rice, and cotton plantations. Because of their isolation from the mainland of Charleston, Beaufort, and Savannah, slaves created their own Creole language called Gullah, and maintained most of their African traditions. Basket making was just one of the African crafts that survived. It is still a lucrative family business in the Gullah communities near Myrtle Beach and Charleston, South Carolina.

*Gullah basket.*

In 1989 a delegation from St. Helena Island, South Carolina, visited Sierra Leone to trace their African roots. They took examples of their baskets. When the Kessee weavers of Sierra Leone saw the Gullah baskets, they were amazed how similar they were to Kessee baskets in weaving and design.

Americans today realize that the enslaved blacksmith, the potter, the seamstress, and others have made many contributions to American civilization through their mastery of skilled handicrafts.

# THREE

## FROM CANVAS TO WALLS

### VISUAL ARTISTS

Can you imagine being forced to create art for someone without pay or recognition because he or she owns you? What would it be like to have to rely on the goodwill and mercy of some rich person to let you paint? What if you weren't allowed to sign your paintings because a law forbade you to read or write? As unreasonable as these restrictions seem today, most slave and free black artists during the eighteenth and early nineteenth centuries had to abide by them.

Because of those slave laws we have only an incomplete picture of African-American art that historians are still scrambling to restore. Their jobs are made more difficult because records of the accomplishments of slaves were not kept by their owners, laws prohibiting slaves from reading and writing were enforced, and their masters believed that slaves were inferior and incapable of producing fine art. Nevertheless, through the study of artistic techniques such as brush strokes, use of color, and subject matter, researchers are beginning to match names with portraits, landscapes, and other visual arts that may have been produced by African-American artists.

During the eighteenth and early nineteenth centuries, only a handful of African-American visual artists received recognition for their works. They include Neptune Thurston, Scipio Moorhead, Moses Williams, Joshua Johnston (Johnson), and Julien Hudson.

**Neptune Thurston** was a slave owned by the famous portrait painter Gilbert Stuart of Newport, Rhode Island. As a boy, Thurston's chalk sketches on barrel heads captured the interest of his master. Though debatable, many people believe Thurston taught Gilbert Stuart how to paint. The best evidence that this may be more than mere folklore is found in an ad in the *Boston Newsletter* (January 7, 1775) that announced the services of a black man who "makes portraits at the lowest rates. . . ." This same ad also hinted that Thurston was trained in Europe like all recognized artists of the period. However, as a black artist, his study in Europe was definitely an exception. Most of his fellow black artists had very limited opportunities for training at home or abroad, and depended almost entirely on secondhand sources for their professional growth. As far as we know, none of Thurston's works survived.

The first African-American painter to receive public recognition was a slave named **Scipio Moorhead**, active in Boston, Massachusetts, during the 1770s. Although owned by Reverend John Moorhead, the painter obviously enjoyed some of the privileges of a free man of color. No doubt he benefited from the instruction and encouragement given him by two very prominent women of Boston—Sarah Moorhead, the wife of his owner and an art teacher who taught Moorhead to draw, and America's first black poet, Phillis Wheatley. Wheatley mentioned Moorhead in her poem "To S.M., A Young African Painter, on seeing His Works," which appeared in her 1773 collection of poems, *Poems on Various Subjects, Religious and Moral*.

While no signed works by Scipio Moorhead survived, art experts are convinced that he produced the famous copperplate engraving of Phillis Wheatley that appeared on most of her published works of poetry.

A third important artist of the period was **Moses Williams**, a silhouettist owned by Charles Willson Peale, a leading artist of the Revolutionary Era.

*Copperplate engraving of Phillis Wheatley, attributed to Scipio Moorhead.*
*1770s. Library of Congress Collection, Washington, D.C.*

Williams is known for his profiles cut on a *physiognotrace*, a device used to draw a reduced-sized outline that the artist would then cut by hand.

For twenty-seven years, Williams worked for Peale in hopes of earning enough money to buy his freedom. His master claimed to be against slavery.

*Silhouettes by Moses Williams. About 1803.*

Yet Peale made up every possible excuse to keep Williams in bondage, including accusing him of being too "lazy" to earn a living. All the while, Williams was getting better and better at cutting silhouettes. By 1803 he had become so skillful that Peale's most prominent patrons actually preferred his profiles over Peale's. Charging eight cents a silhouette, he finally earned enough money to buy a home and marry the Peale's white cook.

None of the early black artists is shrouded in as much mystery as the portraitist **Joshua Johnston,** or **Johnson.** Historians are still trying to figure out his racial background. Was he black or white? The 1817 issue of the Baltimore, Maryland, directory listed Johnston at the end of the register reserved for "Free Householders of Colour," a pretty reliable clue that he probably was, or at least considered himself, an African American.

Johnston's style imitated that of the prominent white portraitists of his time. His stiffly posed subjects showed little personality or emotion. Yet two characteristics of Johnston's paintings distinguished him: He often posed children standing, and he made brass-headed upholstery tacks a part of his compositions. As a result, he came to be known as the "Brass Tacks" artist.

Portrait of a Cleric *(oil on canvas) by Joshua Johnston (Johnson). 1805–1810. Bowdoin College Museum of Art, Brunswick, Maine.*

The majority of Johnston's subjects were wealthy slaveholders and their families. However, he also painted a very impressive portrait of a black man, *Portrait of a Cleric.* Because of the sensitive way in which he painted the black clergyman, art historians believe that Johnston probably painted other African-American subjects as well.

**Julien Hudson**, the only southern artist of the period, was a native of New Orleans. As a member of the free mulatto group there, Hudson was influenced by the flamboyant life-styles of the very wealthy white residents with whom he came in contact. His exposure to the upper class may explain why the subjects in his paintings were all handsomely dressed.

Like Thurston, Hudson was trained in Europe and probably made several trips to France. In 1837 he went to Paris to study under the influential painter Abel de Pujol, who was known for his smoothly finished, detailed, and realistic portraitures. Hudson was greatly influenced by Pujol, and it showed in the quality of his work, especially in his 1838 portrait of Jean Michel Fortier III, a Creole merchant. As described by Patricia Brady in an article in *Who Was Who in African American Art*, "Fortier is shown seated, wearing an elegant dark coat with fashionably stiff collar points and an elaborately tied cravat. His curly, slightly graying dark hair, long sideburns, quizzical brows, and intense dark eyes are emblematic of Creole style."

In 1839, Hudson painted a miniature of a young mulatto man who some historians believe is the artist himself. If that is true, it is the only known self-portrait of an African-American artist in the antebellum period.

## NINETEENTH-CENTURY BLACK ARTISTS

Before the end of the Civil War, and the ratification of the Thirteenth Amendment to the Constitution that abolished slavery in the United States, few black artists were slaves; most were considered free men of color. Slaves gained their freedom in one of three ways: They lived in a state such as Pennsylvania where slavery was abolished in 1780; they purchased their freedom; they were manumitted (set free). Before 1857, New Orleans had one of the largest free black populations in the South. However, freedom did not shield free black artists from racial prejudice or from the attitude that blacks were inferior and incapable of producing fine art. Thus, the biggest hindrance to their careers in the United States was racial discrimination. For this reason, many free black artists decided to live and study in Europe, where they found refuge and respect as professional artists.

The best-known black artists of this period include Robert Scott Duncanson, Edward Mitchell Bannister, Charles Porter, Annie E. Walker, Henry Ossawa Tanner, Robert M. Douglass Jr., and Patrick Reason.

**Robert Scott Duncanson** (1821–1872) was one of the first major African-American painters to achieve national and international recognition and to exhibit his works with white artists. Born in Seneca, New York, to a free black mother and a Scots-Canadian father, Duncanson later moved to Cincinnati, Ohio, where he freely participated in art programs. He began his

Classical Landscape with Ruins, Recollections of Italy *(oil on canvas) by*
*Robert Scott Duncanson. 1854. Howard University Gallery of Art,*
*Washington, D.C.*

career as a landscapist and portraitist. He was inspired by the literature of his time as well as the popular Hudson River School of painting—the first native school of landscape painters in the United States.

In 1839 the Freedmen's Aid Society of Ohio raised money to send Duncanson to Glasgow, Scotland, to study. By 1842 his reputation as a landscapist had skyrocketed. His *Classical Landscape with Ruins, Recollections of Italy* (1854) is part of the Collection of Howard University Gallery of Art.

**Edward Mitchell Bannister** (1828–1901) was born in Canada to a West Indian father and a Canadian mother. Shortly after his birth, the British abolished slavery in all of Canada's provinces, which allowed Bannister the freedom to develop his art. Bannister lost his parents at an early age and moved from relative to relative before settling in Boston in the early 1850s. While in Boston, he discovered the new type of photography called *daguerreotype* (named for French inventor Louis-Jacques-Mandé Daguerre), and saw ways to use photography as an art form.

Bannister's marriage to New York businesswoman Christiana Carteaux enabled him to have his own studio and devote all of his time to painting. He also became an advocate for the Union and the rights of black soldiers during the Civil War. After the war, Bannister and his wife moved to Providence, Rhode Island, where he painted his famous *Under the Oaks* in 1875. Listed as "No. 54—Under the Oaks—E. M. Bannister," this painting was selected for the bronze medal, the highest prize for oil painting, at the 1876 Centennial Exposition, a world's fair held in Philadelphia. But that medal was tarnished by the harsh treatment he received when he went to inquire about it. Bannister related the incident to his friend of thirty years, George W. Whitaker:

"I learned from the newspapers that '54' had received a first-prize medal, so I hurried to the committee rooms to make sure the report was true. As I jostled among them, many resented my presence, some actually commenting within my hearing in a most petulant manner. 'What is that colored person in here for?'" When Bannister finally reached the information desk, the man sitting there questioned, "Well, what do you want here anyway? Speak lively."

"I want to inquire concerning No 54. Is it a prize winner?"

*Approaching Storm (oil on canvas) by Edward Mitchell Bannister. 1886.*
*Smithsonian American Art Museum, Washington, D.C.*
*Gift of G. William Miller.*

"What's that to you?" he said.

"Controlling myself, I said deliberately, 'I am interested in the report that 'Under the Oaks' has received a prize. I painted the picture.'

"An explosion could not have made a more marked impression. Without hesitation he apologized to me, and soon everyone in the room was bowing and scraping to me," Bannister recalled.

As a landscapist, Bannister's paintings draw the viewer into the "sereneness of nature" with picturesque scenes of cottages, sunsets, and streams. Paintings like his *Approaching Storm* are full of movement and passion. Bannister was the only nineteenth-century black artist to stay in America throughout his career.

**Charles E. Porter**, born in Hartford, Connecticut, around 1850, was a talented still-life and landscape painter who found a friend in the famous novelist Mark Twain. Twain, who had lived in Hartford during the 1880s, helped

Still Life with Flowers *(oil on canvas) by Charles E. Porter. 1880s.
Wadsworth Atheneum, Hartford, Connecticut. The Ella Gallup
Sumner and Mary Catlin Sumner Collection Fund.*

Porter get the funds he needed to study and work in Paris, France, by purchasing subscriptions to Porter's paintings. (A subscription was simply an agreement to buy a certain number of paintings, and was a common way of patronizing an artist during the nineteenth century.) Porter also raised money by auctioning his works.

After his studies, Porter opened a studio in Rockville, Connecticut, and became one of the few elite African Americans to make a living as a professional artist. He specialized in painting delicate still lifes and landscapes, which were popular subjects during the Victorian Age.

Little is known about the life or works of **Annie E. Walker**, the only woman painter of the period. She was born in Alabama and graduated from the Cooper Union Art School in New York on May 29, 1895. She later studied at the Academie Julien in Paris. One of the few surviving works by Walker is a charcoal drawing done in the late 1890s, entitled *La Parisienne.*

*La Parisienne (charcoal) by Annie E. Walker. Late 1890s. Howard University Gallery of Art, Washington, D.C.*

At the beginning of his career **Henry Ossawa Tanner** painted what many other African-American artists of the period did—conventional and non-controversial subjects that appealed to their white peers and patrons. Then, while studying in Paris, France, Tanner had a life-changing experience. Trying to live on the proverbial starvation diet of an artist, Tanner nearly died of typhoid fever and had to return to his home in Philadelphia. During his recuperation, he discovered that he was tired of painting the "superficial" Bible scenes so popular in the art world at the time. From that point on, he tapped and capitalized on his experiences as an African American.

Tanner became a pioneer in painting themes about his African-American heritage, and reached into his inner self to develop his unique artistic style of painting where "radiant light played an important role." This technique is especially effective in his famed *Banjo Lesson*, where an old man and child are warmed and lighted by the glow of an unseen hearth fire.

Tanner was born in Pittsburgh, Pennsylvania, in 1859, to devoutly religious parents. His father was a bishop in the African Methodist Episcopal Church, and moved his family to Philadelphia when Henry was seven years old. Another life-changing event occurred when, at seventeen, Tanner visited the 1876 Centennial Exposition in Philadelphia. There, he came across the works of two African-American artists: Edmonia Lewis's *Death of Cleopatra* and Edward M. Bannister's prizewinning landscape, *Under the Oaks*, and decided that it *was* possible to be an artist.

In 1880, Tanner entered the Pennsylvania Academy of Fine Arts, where he was taught and mentored by America's foremost artist and photographer, Thomas Eakins. Tanner was touched by Eakins's dignified portrayal of African Americans, and credited Eakins with inspiring him to continue art as a career. However, his stay at the academy was riddled with insults.

One day Tanner was dragged onto the street by jealous white students, tied to his easel in a mock crucifixion, and left to free himself. This act of cruelty was so terrifying that, years later, he couldn't talk about it without flying into a rage. The experience may account for Tanner's decision to spend most of his professional life in Europe.

The Banjo Lesson *(oil on canvas) by Henry Ossawa Tanner. 1893. Hampton University Museum, Hampton, Virginia.*

At least two black artists of the nineteenth century used their art to openly express anti-slavery beliefs. One of the first to do so was **Robert M. Douglass Jr.** (1809–1887), the son of a West Indian immigrant and a free black woman from Philadelphia. Douglass was educated in the Quaker schools there. While he was accepted in most circles, racial prejudice closed the doors to him as a black artist. Fortunately, a well-known and highly respected white portrait painter, Thomas Sully, looked beyond Douglass's race and saw his potential. Convinced of Douglass's ability, Sully wrote a letter of recommendation for him to study in Europe. However, Douglass's application for a passport to England was denied based on a rule that "people of color are not citizens" and therefore had no right to passports to foreign countries. Somehow Douglass found a way around this discriminatory rule and got to England, where he studied lithography (printmaking).

Douglass later used his art to aid abolitionist leaders such as Frederick Douglass and William Lloyd Garrison. In 1833 the artist created a lithographic portrait of Garrison that he sold for fifty cents a copy to raise funds for the abolitionist movement. Two of his best-known works include a portrait of the president of the Republic of Haiti, Nicholas Fabre Geffrard, and a banner for the Grand Order of Odd Fellows in Philadelphia.

**Patrick Reason** of New York was an important abolitionist artist. Reason attended the African Free School in New York, where he was apprenticed to a white craftsman. While still a student, he created the frontispiece of Charles C. Andrews's *The History of the African Free Schools* (1830). The acknowledgment said, "Engraved from a drawing by P. Reason, a pupil, aged thirteen years." What a boost that must have been for the young black artist!

Reason's most celebrated drawing is a picture of a chained slave with the caption, "Am I not a man and a brother?" This piece soon became the emblem of the British anti-slavery movement and was circulated throughout Europe and the United States.

## EARLY TWENTIETH-CENTURY BLACK ARTISTS

At the turn of the century, blacks saw their rights washed away by a series of Jim Crow Laws (named for a character in a popular minstrel show that depicted African Americans as slothful, dimwitted, and inferior). These repressive laws, which remained in effect into the 1950s, stripped away all the human and civil rights blacks had gained during Reconstruction. As a result, segregation took hold in southern soil like stubborn crabgrass. Everything became segregated: trolleys, schools, hospitals, restaurants, stores, cemeteries. In addition, the Jim Crow Laws took away the African American's right to vote through the initiation of a "poll tax" (blacks had to pay money for the privilege to vote) and "literacy" tests that even a lawyer would find hard to pass.

African Americans were also robbed of their basic right to earn a decent wage, because they were relegated to the most menial, lowest-paid jobs. Worse, lynching of black men, based mostly on false accusations by whites, were carried out in the South almost weekly. The white supremacy group the Ku Klux Klan raided homes and farms, burned crosses in yards, and killed African Americans. Frightened blacks were forced to abandon their homes and move to safety in the North. This movement was called the Great Migration.

The industrial needs of World War I (1914–1918) also lured blacks to New York and other urban centers in the North to fill vacancies in factories left by men going off to war. Harlem was their Mecca, their Promised Land—although Harlem was not always the utopia blacks dreamed it would be. They found some of the same problems they had left behind in the South, namely poor housing, menial labor, and anti-Negro feelings. Nevertheless, the move to Harlem and other urban centers was a period of transformation in the African-American community. According to author Edmund Barry Gaither, "Southern blacks, northern blacks, West Indians and even a few Africans crowded into newly created urban communities, shed their often rural, parochial 19th century selves, and embraced a more aggressive and assertive, more urban and comprehensive identity." Gaither believes that the interaction of blacks from so many cultures fostered the acceptance of African heritage as a shared legacy and led to a cultural and political awakening known as the Harlem Renaissance.

Some historians believe that the Harlem Renaissance actually started in 1900 with the influx of blacks from the South and the Caribbean, but most agree that it began after the end of World War I, around 1919 or 1920. Regardless of the date, the Harlem Renaissance was like the blossoming of a beautiful flower. It opened up opportunities in all aspects of African-American urban life: literature, art, political activity, and performing arts. Though the Harlem Renaissance was centered in New York, it reached into other urban cultural centers such as Washington, D.C., Cleveland, Ohio, and Chicago, Illinois, areas where African Americans had also migrated.

The Harlem Renaissance brought on dramatic changes in the way black artists expressed themselves. Encouraged by Thomas Eakins and other well-established white artists, African Americans broke tradition with the European styles they had long imitated. Buoyed by self-respect and racial pride, they began to express their unique cultural heritage. They cared less about what others thought about them and their art than what they thought about it themselves. It was during the artistic explosion of the Harlem Renaissance that blacks finally received recognition as visual artists.

Oddly enough, **Archibald Motley** (1891–1980), one of the most influential black artists of the Harlem Renaissance period, never lived or worked in Harlem. He was born in New Orleans, Louisiana, but moved to Chicago when he was a young man.

Motley drew inspiration and pleasure from observing urban dwellers in Chicago's South Side having fun, or, as it was called, "good-timing." Because he captured groups of people dancing in clubs, enjoying picnics, and conversing on street corners, he was considered one of the first "action painters." Although Motley never tried to idealize his subjects, he succeeded in making his characters on canvas reflect his own good-humored philosophy. As noted artist Samella Lewis wrote, "Through his works, he reminds us to be good spirited, cheerful and dwell on the bright side of life." Motley's *Chicken Shack,* painted in 1936, is packed with action and good humor.

Another Harlem Renaissance artist whose works were alive with movement was woodcut printer, illustrator, and muralist **Aaron Douglas** (1899–1979). Born and educated in Topeka, Kansas, Douglas's career took off during the heyday of the Harlem Renaissance while he was creating Cubist-type black and white rhythmic illustrations. He was chosen to illus-

Chicken Shack *(oil on canvas) by Archibald Motley Jr. 1936. Harmon Foundation Collection, National Archives, Washington, D.C.*

trate author-philosopher Dr. Alaine Locke's famous book, *The New Negro*. He also illustrated *God's Trombones*, a book of poems, sermons, and verse by James Weldon Johnson.

Black artists of the period were encouraged by the formation of organizations like the Harmon Foundation in the 1920s and the Works Progress Administration (WPA) of the 1930s as well as by the establishment of art departments in historically black colleges that trained and nurtured the brightest African-American artists and provided them with opportunities to exhibit their works.

The Harmon Foundation was founded in 1922 by real estate developer William E. Harmon. His goal: to "recognize and promote the overlooked achievements of African Americans." The foundation gave financial assistance to black artists and organized exhibitions of their works across the United States. The WPA was created in 1935 under President Franklin D. Roosevelt's New Deal to provide useful work for the millions of people affected by the Great Depression (1929–1939). At a time when the artist community was losing patrons, this government agency took up the slack by commissioning or paying black artists to work on certain art projects or exhibits. Thus the skills, dignity, and self-respect of these artists were preserved. The Federal Art Project, Federal Writers' Project, and the Federal Theatre Project were all offsprings of the WPA and created thousands of jobs for artists, writers, and actors who were paid to create work for public buildings, document local life, and organize community theaters.

Although the Nineteenth Amendment to the U.S. Constitution, passed in 1920, had given women the right to vote, the doors of opportunity did not swing as wide for them as for men. But several African-American women did make their mark. One of the most prominent women of the period was **Laura Wheeler Waring** (1887–1948), a painter known for portraiture.

Born in Hartford, Connecticut, Waring attended the Pennsylvania Academy of Fine Arts and later studied in Paris and was awarded a scholarship in Europe. When she returned to the United States, she took a job as an instructor at Cheyney State Teachers College in Pennsylvania.

Waring's realistic style of painting was closely related to the work of the rebellious French Romantics of the late eighteenth and nineteenth centuries. However, she quickly departed from the stiffness of the Romantic school to form her own identity as a painter. The Romantic artists emphasized human rights and the value of individual differences in their portrayal of people. As the famous French philosopher Jean Jacques Rousseau once said, "I may be no better than anyone else; but at least I'm different." For Romantics it was

*Frankie (oil) by Laura Wheeler Waring. 1937. Harmon Foundation Collection, National Archives, Washington, D.C.*

an honor to be different. Two examples of Waring's new style can be seen in *Frankie* (1937) and a lifelike portrait of *Anne Washington Derry.*

## THE 1950s AND BEYOND

Unrest is one word that sums up the political atmosphere in the United States from the 1950s to the 1970s. The Korean and Vietnam wars were fought; landmark Supreme Court cases such as *Brown* v. *Board of Education* forced the integration of schools; the civil rights movement resulted in protests like the well-publicized March on Washington. The 1960s was also a decade of tragedy as Americans witnessed the assassination of President John F. Kennedy, his brother Senator Robert Kennedy, Dr. Martin Luther King Jr., and Malcolm X. Black people were so outraged by the assassinations of their leaders that they took to the streets in protest. Unfortunately, the protests turned into riots that destroyed black communities such as Watts in Los Angeles, California, and the 14th Street Corridor in Washington, D.C.

Out of these seemingly chaotic conditions grew at least one group of black artists, AfriCobra (Coalition of Black Revolutionary Artists). Founded by militant black artists, this group, now called the African Commune of Bad Relevant Artists, sought to explore and express racial pride and the African-American aesthetic in one voice. Its members believed that there are qualities that are specific to African people and that these qualities can be expressed by the use of "bright colors, the human figure, lost and found lines, lettering, and images which identify the social," writes Samella Lewis.

Retired Howard University dean of fine art professor and artist **Dr. Jeff Donaldson** was one of the founding members of AfriCobra, and today lectures nationally on what the organization contributed and continues to contribute to art. Like his colleagues, Donaldson produces art that communicates positive thoughts about the African-American experience. The

Victory in the Valley of Eshu *(mixed media) by Jeff Donaldson. 1971. Artist's collection.*

*The Wall of Respect. 1967. Destroyed.*

group's philosophy is reflected in Donaldson's 1971 *Victory in the Valley of Eshu*. In this composition, Donaldson uses what Samella Lewis describes as "singing, Kool-Aid colors of orange, strawberry, cherry, lemon, lime and grape to capture the colors of the sun and of nature."

The search for a black identity and the expression of black militancy during the 1950s and 1960s could not always be confined to canvas. Instead, the black artists often expressed themselves through murals painted on the sides of buildings in urban ghettos. The most famous of these murals was *The*

*Wall of Respect* in Chicago, which celebrated "Black Heroes." Painted on the side of a building by members of the Visual Arts Workshop of the Organization of Black American Culture in 1967, this mural inspired an outdoor mural movement that grew to more than one thousand murals in ethnic communities around the country.

Author Edmund Barry Gaither said, "*The Wall of Respect* is regarded by many as the spiritual source of the black art movement in the visual arts." However, because the area around the wall was condemned as unsafe and eventually torn down, the only visual evidence that's left of this monumental mural is a photograph.

## SPANNING THE TWENTIETH CENTURY

The tradition of excellence in black visual arts begun during the Harlem Renaissance continued into the late 1990s—and even today. Hale Woodruff, Jacob Lawrence, Romare Bearden, Elizabeth Catlett, Samella Lewis, John Biggers, Ellis Wilson, and Lois Mailou Jones are just a few giants whose contributions stand as monuments on the landscape of American art.

Many of these late-twentieth-century visual artists shared more than their art. Some taught art or established art departments at historically black colleges, lived and worked in Africa and the Caribbean, and broke down barriers of prejudice by organizing successful annual exhibits of African-American art.

One such artist was **Hale Woodruff** (1900–1980). Woodruff faced many setbacks and hardships in trying to complete his education at the Herron Art Institute in Indianapolis, Indiana. Nevertheless, he persevered and became one of America's most highly respected art professors, abstract artists, and muralists. Woodruff's most noted murals, created between 1938–1939 at Talladega College, a small black college near Atlanta, Georgia, are of the *Amistad* mutiny trials in Connecticut. To add authenticity to his murals, Woodruff conducted exhaustive research at the Yale University Library where he found photographs of all the participants in the African slave ship trial.

Of even greater prominence was **Jacob Lawrence** (1917–2000), a narrative painter whose career spanned more than sixty years. At age twenty-one, Lawrence had already received national recognition, but his big break came

The Migration of the Negro *(mural), Panel 1, "During the World War there was a great migration North by Southern Negroes," by Jacob Lawrence. 1940–1941. The Phillips Collection, Washington, D.C.*

two years later when he applied his storytelling ability to create a mural called *The Migration of the Negro*. This series of sixty boldly colored panels chronicles the movement of blacks from the rural South to the urban North in search of jobs and hope. *Migration* was sold soon after completion in 1941. The even-numbered panels went to the New York Museum of Modern Art,

The Survivor *(linocut)*
*by Elizabeth Catlett.*
*1983. Hampton*
*University Museum,*
*Hampton, Virginia.*

and the odd-numbered panels went to the Phillips Collection in Washington. However, both collections have been reunited several times for exhibitions.

Artist, educator, army veteran, musician, and author **Romare Bearden** (1912–1988) was a late-blooming artist. While he knew in his heart that art was his calling, he had difficulty finding his stylistic place. In his search, Bearden worked as a cartoonist for the *Baltimore Afro-American* newspaper, and as a musician and songwriter. Finally, he found his niche as a collage artist in 1964, and by 1971 the Museum of Modern Art in New York gave him a retrospective show that won him national recognition.

**Elizabeth Catlett** (1915– ) is both a contemporary sculptor and print-maker. In both mediums, she expresses the struggle of her people. "She therefore brings to the art world a social consciousness. . . ." states the author of *African-Americans in the Visual Arts: A Historical Perspective.*

Catlett herself has experienced the pain of discrimination. Even though she passed the entrance exam, she was denied admission to the Carnegie Institute of Technology in 1932 because of her race. Instead she entered Howard University where she studied under Lois Mailou Jones. In 1940 Catlett enrolled at the State University of Iowa and became the first student to receive a M.F.A. degree there.

In the 1960s, Catlett settled permanently in Cuernavaca, Mexico. Among her many celebrated linocuts is the strong image of a resolute black woman entitled *The Survivor*, painted in 1983.

"From four years old I was drawing," recalled **Samella Lewis** (1925– ) in an interview with the *Richmond Times Dispatch* in February 1977. She explained that she found subjects for her artistic reinterpretations in many things from comic books to police brutality against blacks to her older sister's romance books. Lewis's long career has been multifaceted. She is a painter,

The Word *by Samella Lewis. 1995. Artist's collection.*

graphic artist, educator, and author. In 1975, Lewis cofounded *Black Art: An International Quarterly* as a means of getting art into the homes of African Americans who would not ordinarily have it or be exposed to it.

Still working, still exhibiting, still writing, this prolific artist and writer continues to be productive because as she puts it, "I can't stop. . . ." A recent work called *The Word* (1995) is a vibrant church scene in which a Bible-waving preacher, clothed in white, delivers his message to an attentive flock.

Muralist **John Biggers** (1924– ) has been a one-man show most of his life, experimenting with drafting, lithography, sculpture, and painting in a variety of mediums. He is also a philosopher and art teacher.

Biggers adheres to the Mexican concept of the mural as an educational tool. Thus his mission is to use his art to educate impoverished people of their history and to reflect the value of the African-American experience. His 1987 mural *Song of the Drinking Gourds* (acrylic on prepared plaster over concrete), which is painted on the Senior Citizen Craft House in Tom Bass Regional Park outside Houston, Texas, resembles a giant quilt hanging in the open air.

 **Ellis Wilson** (1899–1971) had to leave his Kentucky birthplace to find himself as an artist. A study tour to Haiti helped him find his way. He drew inspiration from the quiet dignity of the Haitian people as they went about their daily activities. Not until 1949 did Wilson gain recognition by his home-town. In that year a one-man show was mounted at the Graves County Library, and a series of articles in the *Courier-Journal* (Louisville, Kentucky) featured his work. At fifty years old, Wilson finally received his just reward. He recalled that this was one of the highlights of his life. Wilson's most popular work, *Haitian Funeral Procession*, was painted about 1950.

Born in Boston, Massachusetts, in 1905, **Lois Mailou Jones** is a giant among giants and a strong advocate of excellence in African-American art. Jones was one of the first black graduates of the Boston Museum School of Fine Arts. Later, she taught at Howard University where she nurtured and guided numerous young students to artistic maturity.

Jones's career spanned sixty years, and, during that time, her artistic style changed dramatically. Her earlier works, as seen in *Negro Boy* (1935, watercolor), reflect a realistic, yet dignified style. Later she incorporated Cubism

Les Fetiches *(oil on linen) by Lois Mailou Jones. 1938.*
*Smithsonian American Art Museum, Washington, D.C.*

and African and Haitian art to express her African heritage. All three influences are readily seen in her *Les Fetiches*.

The collective works of the unsung as well as the celebrated black artists tell the story, not only of the African-American struggle for emancipation from slavery, but also from artistic restrictions that lasted two centuries.

# FOUR

# ETCHED IN STONE

## AFRICAN-AMERICAN SCULPTORS

Africans arrived on the shores of the Americas already knowing how to create objects out of wood, stone, bronze, iron, and gold—the natural and abundant resources of their native lands. Their background included world masterpieces such as the ancient Benin and Ife bronzes. The famous Spanish artist Pablo Picasso once declared that African sculpture "has never been surpassed."

The artistic ability as sculptors that African slaves brought with them to America was further honed in the shops of white men, particularly abolitionists under whom they served as apprentices. Eugene Warburg, (Mary) Edmonia "Wildfire" Lewis, Meta Vaux Warrick Fuller, Sargeant Claude Johnson, Augusta Fells Savage, and Selma Burke are among a very small number of recognized black sculptors whose careers spanned the nineteenth and early twentieth centuries.

**Eugene Warburg** (1825–1867) was born free in New Orleans, Louisiana. He was the son of Daniel Warburg, a member of a distinguished German Jewish family, and Marie Rose Blondeau, the elder Warburg's Cuban mulatto slave. Shortly after Marie Rose gave birth to Eugene, Warburg freed and married her. The couple had four other children.

Eugene Warburg's mulatto status and his father's connections opened doors for him that would have been closed to most blacks. After a brief period making funerary sculpture and tombs, he decided to go abroad and study sculpture under Philippe Garbeille, a French sculptor most noted for his busts of well-known personalities. The irony is that Eugene financed his trip through the sale of three slaves left from his mother's estate.

With help from his father's friend, Pierre Soule, a prominent lawyer from France and U.S. minister to Spain, Eugene received a commission to do a sculpture of John Young Mason. Soule persuaded sixty American businessmen in Paris to contribute to Warburg's commission with Mason. Warburg completed the classical marble bust of Mason in August 1855, and it was placed in the Beaux Arts section of the Universal Exposition. Mason was very pleased, calling the rendition a "faithful representation."

John Young Mason
*(marble) by Eugene Warburg. 1855. Virginia Historical Society, Richmond.*

**(Mary) Edmonia "Wildfire" Lewis** (1843?–1900?), the daughter of a Chippewa Indian mother and a free black father, was the first African-American woman artist to be recognized as a sculptor. Lewis studied at Oberlin College, but while there she was often harassed by her white classmates. Unable to concentrate on her studies, she left Oberlin and moved to Boston, where abolitionist leader and newspaper editor William Lloyd Garrison arranged for her to study with a noted sculptor, Edward A. Brackett. Lewis set up a small studio and began to create clay and plaster medallions of Garrison, John Brown, and other notable anti-slavery personalities.

During the Civil War, Lewis created a bust of Colonel Robert Gould Shaw, the commander of the first black regiment raised in Massachusetts. Shortly after the war, she sculpted *Forever Free* (1867). It depicts a slave bursting from chains and was the first sculpture by an African American to celebrate the Emancipation Proclamation. These two highly acclaimed works brought Lewis national recognition.

Lewis was among the few privileged African Americans to exhibit at the historic 1876 Centennial Exposition in Philadelphia. She exhibited seven pieces of sculpture at the Exposition, but the piece that caused the greatest stir was *The Death of Cleopatra*. In other contemporary sculptures of the famous Egyptian queen, Cleopatra was depicted as calm, idealized, and regal. Lewis's piece dramatically broke with accepted standards to show an anguished, dying queen. "The effects of death are represented with such skill as to be absolutely repellant," wrote New York artist William J. Clark Jr. in his *Great American Sculptures* (1878). For many years, this piece of sculpture was thought to be lost, but luckily it was found in Chicago in 1989.

In their book on African-American artists, Romare Bearden and Harry Henderson described Lewis as a pioneer in the field of sculpture, writing, "In courageous men and women who fought against slavery, in women like Hagar and Harriot Hunt who struggled against the oppression and suffering of women, in the spirituality of Native Americans, and ultimately in her religious faith, Lewis found her great themes. . . . She is a heroic and legendary figure in American art."

The Death of Cleopatra *by (Mary) Edmonia Lewis. 1875. Smithsonian American Art Museum, Washington, D.C. Gift of the Historical Society of Forest Park, IL.*

Another African-American woman who had a tremendous impact on black art was **Meta Vaux Warrick Fuller** (1877–1968). Warrick Fuller was born in Philadelphia, Pennsylvania, to middle-class parents who introduced her to museums at an early age. They were collectors of art themselves.

Warrick Fuller showed great aptitude for art, and passed a strenuous exam for a scholarship to the Pennsylvania Museum School of Industrial Arts (Pennsylvania Academy of Fine Arts). At graduation, she won first prize for a metal crucifix of Christ and honorable mention for a clay model she called *Procession of Arts and Crafts*. In 1899 she enrolled at the Colarossi Academy in Paris, and met the great European sculptor Rodin. When Rodin saw Warrick Fuller's sculpture *Secret Sorrow*, he remarked, "Mademoiselle, you are a sculptor; you have the sense of form in your fingers." What a great compliment coming from the creator of the famous *Thinker.*

The Awakening of Ethiopia *(plaster) by Meta Warrick Fuller. 1914. Schomburg Center, New York City.*

Most of Warrick Fuller's works incorporated African and Egyptian themes and the African-American experience that was started by Edmonia Lewis. In 1907, Warrick Fuller was commissioned by the Jamestown Tercentennial Exposition to create a sculpture showing the history of blacks in America. She created two works for the Tercentennial: *The Awakening of Ethiopia* and *Mary Turner* to memorialize both the actual and symbolic lynching of black women and their struggle for equality, self-definition, and freedom.

Among the most successful sculptors of the Harlem Renaissance was **Sargent Claude Johnson** (1887–1967), who was born in Boston. During his career, Johnson experimented with the styles of many different cultures, but African and Mexican styles were his main interests. In 1928, *Sammy*, one of several noted ceramic busts created by Johnson, was entered in a Harmon Foundation exhibition and won the coveted Otto H. Kahn prize.

Johnson captured human emotion in his sculptures. More than any other black artist of the period, he seemed to be able to express his art verbally and visually. He was quoted in the *San Francisco Chronicle* (October 6, 1935) as saying, "It is the pure American Negro I am concerned with, aiming to show the natural beauty and dignity in that characteristic lip and that characteristic hair, bearing and manner; and I wish to show that beauty not so much to the White man as to the Negro himself." *Standing Woman* aptly conveys this philosophy.

Standing Woman *(terracotta) by Sargent Claude Johnson. 1934. Fine Arts Museum of San Francisco.*

The influence and accomplishments of **Augusta Fells Savage** (1900–1962) have been undervalued in African-American art. Born in Green Cove Springs, Florida, the seventh of fourteen children of a strict Methodist minister, Augusta discovered her love for modeling clay when she was six years old, at "the mud pie age." Unfortunately her father did not understand her drive to create art, for he felt the little clay farm animals she made were graven images against the Lord. But young Augusta's talent could not be suppressed. By the time she entered secondary school, her ability to sculpt was so advanced that she was asked to teach her fellow classmates.

Savage exhibited her sculptures at county fairs, and the more portraits she did for local people, the more money she earned. But Savage was not satisfied; she was determined to move to New York and study there. She did so in 1920. In a year she was studying sculpture under George Brewster at Cooper Union.

"Even before she completed her four-year course of study at Cooper Union, Savage had gained fame for a portrait of W.E.B. Du Bois," note the editors of *African American Women Artists*. The bust of Du Bois boosted Savage's reputation, and she quickly became the artistic "belle" of Harlem. She also won a scholarship for summer study at the prestigious Palace of Fountainbleau art school in France. However, when officials learned that she was black, the scholarship money was withdrawn with an apology. Her rejection made front-page news in the radical black press. Unfortunately it also earned Savage the reputation of an agitator and she was rebuffed by the white art world.

Savage became a community activist and sacrificed her own art career to teach and help other artists. She established several studios in Harlem where she taught children and youth who could not afford art lessons. In 1932 she founded the Savage Studio of Arts and Crafts in Harlem. In a very astute move, Savage managed to affiliate her school with the State University of New York, making it the largest art school of its kind in New York. In addition, she helped to organize the Harlem Artist Guild and a club called the Vanguard to support black artists and inform them of the issues confronting them.

Lift Every Voice and Sing, *or* The Harp *(plaster)*
*by Augusta Fells Savage. 1939. Destroyed.*
*Courtesy Schomburg Center, New York City.*

Savage's 1929 bronze sculpture, *Gamin*, won her a fellowship scholarship from the Julius Fund to study in Paris. "Gaming" was the word used for hundreds of mischievous urban ghetto youth who roamed the streets. Savage's bronze bust of a young lad captures the essence of the young boy's personality. Wearing a "bebop" cap with its wide brim cocked to one side, the figure tilts his head in the same direction and looks past the observer. The boy's disheveled appearance contributes to the sculpture's informality and immediate appeal. In 1939, Savage created a 16-foot (4.8-meter) plaster sculpture called *Lift Every Voice and Sing*, or *The Harp*, for the New York World's Fair to honor author and composer James Weldon Johnson, a fellow Floridian. This massive sculpture also paid homage to the musical heritage of African Americans. The composition featured a group of African-American singers arranged in the shape of a harp.

Even less celebrated than Augusta Savage but just as influential was **Selma Burke** (1900–1995). An essayist for *Women Artists of Color* suggests that Burke's life is the stuff of mythology, and that the artist had no small hand in the creation and maintenance of that legend. By all accounts, Burke was a self-promoting black woman who made it her business to interact with art legends such as Pablo Picasso and Georgia O'Keeffe.

Like Savage, Burke was born in the South. While playing with the clay her mother collected for whitewash from

*Jim (plaster) by Selma Burke. 1935. Schomburg Center, New York City.*

the local creek near her family's farm in Mooresville, North Carolina, she got her first inkling that she wanted to be a sculptor. She said, "It was there in 1907 that I discovered me."

From 1938 to 1939, Burke studied sculpture under Aristide Maillol in Paris and with ceramist Michael Povoleny in Vienna. Upon her return to the United States, she attended college, receiving a Masters of Fine Arts from Columbia University and a doctorate in arts and letters from Riverstone College in Salisbury, North Carolina. But she never gave up her love of sculpting, often supporting her art studies by serving as a model. Her modeling work led to a fellowship that enabled her to go back to Europe.

Burke's best-known sculptural portrait, a bronze plaque bearing the bust profile of President Franklin D. Roosevelt, became the model for Roosevelt's likeness on the U.S. dime in 1946. She won the commission in 1943, and had the audacity to write the president the following letter:

> *Dear Mr. President:*
> *During the lifetime of President George Washington, the French sculptor, Houdon, was invited to come to this country. He traveled two months by boat. As you perhaps saw in the newspapers, I won the competition to do your bust. I live one hour by plane, two by railroad, and four by car. May I have a sitting with you?*

President Roosevelt was quick to oblige the plucky artist. Her original portrait is now on exhibit at the Recorder of Deeds Building in Washington, D.C.

While at Columbia, Burke became a good friend of fellow student Margo Einstein, daughter of Albert Einstein. The Einsteins became her staunchest supporters. An early, undated plaster sculpture, *Jim*, is an excellent example of her skill and of the vigor and nobility she gave her subjects. As author Crystal A. Britton states, "The artist's sensitivity to issues is transmitted through her sculpture."

The same can be said for all these early sculptors who transmitted their culture and the beauty of the human spirit through their images.

# FIVE

# PRIMITIVE ON PURPOSE

## FOLK ARTISTS

Art collector Dr. Regenia A. Perry defines folk art as "those art forms created by persons with no formal artistic training." Other experts describe folk, naive, and primitive art as art that's outside the acceptable "canons," or standards, but inseparable from daily life. Still other scholars say that there is no pat definition of folk art, no set criteria. All would agree that folk art has one thing in common—it is made by folk for folk.

Folk artists are often called nonconformists, because they are not in the business of imitating anyone or any art style. As young people say, "They keep it real." The reason they can "keep it real" is that they don't have to answer to art dealers or have anyone tell them what to create. They are often unknown and self-taught; are isolated in rural areas; are late starters; are guided or inspired by visions from God; and are unaffected by what people think about them or their art. And, though their works have been labeled by the so-called "insiders" as "outsider art," "naive," "primitive," "visionary," they are perhaps the purest interpreters of American life and culture.

Folk art has had a tremendous impact on mainstream artists, both black and white. In many ways it resembles the works of early European modern artists like Pablo Picasso, Henri Matisse, and Paul Klee who also rejected

**64**

formal training to try to achieve the intensity of the folk artist. It is well known that Picasso was influenced by African art. His "bold distortions of human figures" are based on his fascination with and study of African masks.

Folk artists have defined or created themselves, and continue to tell their stories on canvases and wood, in sculptures of stone, wire, and other found objects, and in carvings. There are two distinct groups of folk artists: the self-taught and those who are trained, but are inspired to abandon their formal training for the simpler, more expressive art form. As with all the other art genres, the list of great African-American folk artists is much too long to mention every name in this book. However, from among the discovered and undiscovered, a few stand out; some of them self-taught and others "primitive on purpose."

## AFRICAN-AMERICAN FOLK ARTISTS

Initially self-taught, **Palmer Hayden** (1893–1973) received training in New York and Paris. Born on January 15, 1893, in Widewater, Virginia, Hayden was christened Peyton Cole Hedgeman. He later changed his name to Palmer Hayden, the signature that appears on all his paintings. Hayden received his first training through a drawing correspondence course he took while in the army during World War I. When he was discharged, he moved to New York so he could continue his studies, while working parttime to support himself.

In 1925, Hayden spent time in Boothbay, Maine, a seaport town. While studying at the Boothbay Art Colony, Hayden received a working scholarship that allowed him to continue to perfect his art. The coastal environment inspired Hayden to paint boats and marine subjects. In 1926 he exhibited his seascapes at the Civic Club in New York. These paintings won him two Harmon Foundation awards, a gold medal, and a cash prize of $400. With the award money and funds from a loyal patron, Hayden sailed for Paris to study at the prestigious Ecole des Beaux Arts.

Although Hayden received thorough academic training in New York, Maine, and Paris, his works always retained a naive character that he developed as a youngster. Then, during the 1930s, Hayden perfected a "consciously naive" style. He also made the decision to paint African-American

The Janitor Who Paints *(oil) by Palmer Hayden. About 1937.*
*Smithsonian American Art Museum, Washington, D.C.*
*Gift of the Harmon Foundation.*

themes exclusively. He specialized in capturing black people at their most unguarded and natural moments, as portrayed in *The Janitor Who Paints*.

Folk sculptor **William Edmondson** (1882–1951) was born one of six children in Davidson County, Tennessee, to former slave parents. After years of working first for the railroad and then for a women's hospital, Edmondson became a stone mason. Then he entered the world of art. Operating on what he felt was a divine command from God, Edmondson was "called" to carve just as a preacher in the African-American tradition is sometimes "called" to preach the gospel. "While he lay asleep, God appeared at the head of his bed and talked to him, like a natural man, concerning the talent of cutting stone He was about to bestow." Edmondson told a reporter for the Nashville *Tennessean*, "He talked so loud He woke me up. He told me He had something for me." Edmondson was told to make chisels and other sculpting tools.

Crucifixion *(carved limestone) by William Edmondson. About 1932–1937. Smithsonian American Art Museum, Washington, D.C. Gift of Elizabeth Gibbons-Hanson.*

Edmondson created very compact statues that resembled African sculpture. Most of his early works were created as gravestones, figurative sculptures, and garden ornaments. Edmondson worked exclusively in limestone that came from demolished buildings and curbs from rebuilt streets. Wrecking companies often deposited loads of limestone in his backyard at no cost. During the fifty-plus years Edmondson sculpted, his backyard was filled with a menagerie of what he called his "mirkels" (miracles): preachers, doves, angels, rabbits, turtles, and other critters.

Five years after he began to sculpt, he was "discovered" by a photographer for *Harper's Bazaar* magazine, Dahl-Wolfe. The photographer recommended Edmondson to Alfred Barr, the director of the Museum of Modern Art in New York, who was interested in the so-called "modern primitive" style that they applied to Edmondson's sculpture. As a consequence, Edmondson became the first African-American artist to be accorded a one-man show at the museum. His *Crucifixion* (1932–1937) celebrates Christ as Savior.

Born in Florence, South Carolina, on March 18, 1901, **William Henry Johnson** was a trained artist who effectively employed a variety of styles—academic, Impressionism, Cubism, German Expressionism, and finally "conscious naiveté."

Johnson dropped out of school at an early age so he could help support his family, but as a child he enjoyed copying cartoons from local newspapers—an activity that may have developed his ability to tell stories through pictures. In 1921, Johnson enrolled at the National Academy of Design, where he worked with the renowned painter Charles W. Hawthorne. Later, with help from Hawthorne, he went to Europe to study. While in Europe, Johnson traveled widely. He visited Corsica, Nice in France, Belgium, and Denmark. He was impressed with the Impressionist movement, but the works that excited him most were those done by the Expressionists, particularly Chaim Soutine. Johnson tried his hand at Expressionism.

In 1930, Johnson exhibited some of his works in a Harmon Foundation show and received a gold medal. He then returned to Europe and married Danish textile artist Holcha Krake, whom he had met earlier in France. But soon the threat of World War II prompted Johnson to return to the United

Folk Family *(oil on wood) by William Henry Johnson. About 1939–1940. Smithsonian American Art Museum, Washington, D.C. Gift of the Harmon Foundation.*

States in 1938. His return to the United States "marked a pronounced and unexpected change in his style of painting," says Dr. Regenia A. Perry. Johnson became interested in religious subjects, and these were almost always African Americans. His style changed, too. "Using a palette of only four or five colors and painting frequently on burlap or plywood, Johnson developed a flat, consciously naive style," explains Dr. Perry. A prime example is Johnson's *Folk Family* (1939–1940), which portrays real African-American folks doing ordinary things.

Several books have been written about the revered folk artist **Clementine Hunter** (1886–1988), whose life spanned a century. When she was around five years old, her parents moved to a plantation in the Cane River region of Louisiana, an area that supported the Creole culture to which Clementine belonged. "All my people were Creoles. They say us Creoles got more different kinds of blood than any other people. When I was growing up all the folks on lower Cane River were Creoles . . . spoke nothing but French," she remarked in an interview with James L. Wilson, author of *Clementine Hunter, American Folk Artist*.

Hunter was never very interested in school and kept running away. Since her parents needed her to help with the work, they didn't force her to return. At about fourteen, Hunter's family moved again, this time to nearby Melrose Plantation, the subject of most of her paintings. As Samella Lewis writes, "Instead of bending to the problems of life, Hunter used her art to lend dig-

Baptizing *(oil on paperboard) by Clementine Hunter. About 1950.*
*Fisk University Museum, Nashville, Tennessee.*

nity to her community of people." Therefore, she frequently painted ordinary folks living everyday normal lives.

Hunter's *Baptizing* depicts the ceremony surrounding the baptism of a child in the rural South. Hunter was illiterate, but learned to copy the initials of Cammy Henry, the owner of the plantation. Thinking that she might cause confusion by using her employer's initials, she made the C backward. Later she made her marks even more her own by placing the C over the H, which became her unique signature.

John Brown Going to His Hanging *(oil on canvas) by Horace Pippin. 1942. The Pennsylvania Academy of the Fine Arts, Philadelphia. John Lambert Fund.*

**Horace Pippin** was also a self-taught artist who, even when given the opportunity for formal training, rejected it after a short while for the primitive style. Like most folk artists, Pippin drew on personal experiences.

Pippin was born in Pennsylvania but grew up in Goshen, New York. His father died when he was young, and he had to quit school at fifteen to take care of his sick mother. In 1911, Pippin moved to New Jersey, and during World War I, enlisted in the army. He was wounded in France and suffered partial paralysis of his right arm. Determined not to let a disability get in the way of his art, Pippin developed an exercise to strengthen his arm. In 1929, Pippin began painting war memories. In 1942, he painted his famous *John Brown Going to His Hanging.*

*Let's Make a Record (tempera, acrylic, and pencil on paperboard) by Sister Gertrude Morgan. About 1978. Smithsonian American Art Museum, Washington, D.C. Gift of Chuck and Jan Rosenak.*

The colorful **Sister Gertrude Morgan** (1900–1980) was born in Alabama, but moved to New Orleans in 1957. There she became a street evangelist, singer, and guitarist, but gave up street preaching to spread the gospel through art. Sister Morgan began dressing in all white after claiming to get a message from God telling her she was the bride of Christ. In her painting *Let's Make a Record*, Sister Morgan, dressed in her signature white, is seated on a throne-like chair and surrounded by a host of angels. Two scribbled Bible verses appear above her head and shoulders.

## CONTEMPORARY FOLK ARTISTS

"Art ain't about paint. It ain't about canvas. It's about ideas," says **Thorton Dial Sr.** (1928– ), a contemporary sculptor and painter. His main goal is to use his art to express what's on his mind. "Too many people died without

King of Africa *(enamel, carpet, and industrial sealing compound on wood) by Thorton Dial Sr. 1989. Private collection.*

ever getting their mind out to the world. I have found how to get my ideas out and I won't stop," he said.

Dial has spent his life using his skill as a steelworker to make "things"—mostly out of scrap metal. At age fifty-five, after working thirty years for the Pullman Standard Company, makers of railroad cars, Dial found himself out of work. Although he had little education and absolutely no art training, he then began to devote more and more time to creating sculptures and paintings. According to Sandra Kraskin, curator of the exhibit *Wrestling with History: A Celebration of African American Self-Taught Artists,* "Thornton Dial, Sr., does not decorate objects. He wrestles with history and tradition, challenging the boundary between self-taught and contemporary mainstream art."

Dial's powerful and colorful images use the trickster tiger, the strong and dominating animal that outwits and controls other animals in many African folk tales, to portray African-American men struggling to achieve equality in a white-dominated society. His 1989 *King of Africa* is on exhibit at Virginia Union University in Richmond, Virginia.

Folk artist **Ana Bel Lee** (1924–2000), who lived on St. Simons Island, Georgia, for sixteen years after a long career as a social worker in Detroit, Michigan, used her canvas to tell stories of her heritage and culture. Lee found her spirit on St. Simons Island, and a free spirit it was. Her vibrant paintings of low-country life have a powerful attraction. Most portray historical events in African-American history, but some depict ordinary events like weddings, Saturday baths in tin tubs, and going to church and festivals.

Lee has been criticized for dressing her black people in their Sunday finest rather than showing them in everyday clothing. "All the pictures I'd seen of southern blacks showed them as raggedy, so I decided my people would be dressed nice. I dress them as they could have been," she explained in several newspaper interviews.

One of her most provocative paintings is of the slave rebellion that ended in suicide at Ibo Landing on St. Simons Island, which some criticize for not being historically accurate. Done in two panels, the first panel shows the captured Africans as defiant, some still standing on the banks of Dunbar Creek on St. Simons Island and others almost totally submerged. The second panel depicts them coming ashore in Africa.

"Historians see the slaves going into the water, but I see them coming up out of the water in Africa. It's my way of showing hope," she explained.

# SIX

# CAUGHT ON CAMERA

## BLACK PHOTOGRAPHERS

Revolution is a word often associated with war, but Frenchman Louis Daguerre caused a revolution of a different sort back in 1839. He revolutionized photography with a new process called *daguerreotype* that consisted of treating silver-plated copper sheets with iodine to make them sensitive to light, then exposing them in a camera, and "developing" the images with warm mercury vapor.

Daguerreotypes brought affordable photography within reach of the common person. For about two dollars, a person in almost any town "could be immortalized on a slip of silver, framed with a rich gilt mat, and pressed into a fitted case covered in fine embossed leather," writes an authority at the Daguerreian Society's Web site.

A few months after Daguerre's process was announced in Paris, a ship carrying the full details arrived in New York, bringing with it new career opportunities for African Americans. By 1840 blacks (and whites) were making photographs in studios all across the country, but mostly in northern cities.

The fairly inexpensive and easy-to-use equipment needed attracted blacks to this type of photography. Plus, there was a growing demand from blacks to have their images preserved. Blacks had grown weary of the "watermelon eating darkie" image of African Americans popularized in minstrel flyers, broadsides, and advertisements in the mid-nineteenth century. Daguerreotypes and other cheaper forms of photography such as the tintypes, ambrotypes, and stereotypes gave black photographers the ammunition to change the image of black people. They could use the new technology to show a dignified, proud, and ambitious race of people, and they did!

A free black, **Jules Lion** (1810–1866) was the first recorded daguerreotypist in New Orleans. Lion studied lithography in France and received an honorable mention for a lithograph at the Paris Exposition in 1833.

In the summer of 1839, Jules discovered the daguerreotype process. Recognizing photography's money-making potential, by September of that same year he was back in New Orleans showing daguerreotypes. Lion became a local celebrity and received widespread and favorable newspaper coverage.

For the next twenty-five years, Jules Lion worked from his studio in New Orleans, capturing its beautiful architecture and the life of its people—rich and poor.

## MID-NINETEENTH-CENTURY PHOTOGRAPHERS

**James Presley Ball** (1825–1904) learned the daguerreotype process in 1840 from African-American photographer John B. Bailey of Boston. One of Ball's earliest works is a half-plate daguerreotype of a group of men in top hats standing before a confectionery. This photograph, like most of Ball's works, is enclosed in a brass mat and embossed with his name, J. P. Ball/Cincinnati.

On New Year's Day in 1851, Ball opened his first successful studio, employing his brothers and his brother-in-law as well as the famous landscapist Robert S. Duncanson, who hand tinted some of Ball's 1850s photographs. By 1854, Ball employed nine men, including one white man, and was earning as much as $100 a day. While few of his images of African Americans survived, there is a family album that contains sensitive *cartes des visite* (postcards) of his grandmother, brothers, in-laws, and nieces and nephews.

**Augustus Washington** was born free in Trenton, New Jersey, in 1820 or 1821 to an Asian mother and African father. As a free child of color, Augustus attended private school with white students. However, by 1830 whites were anxious about the growing abolitionist movement and passed laws and ordinances to restrict the movement of free blacks and rescind the rights they had been given. As one writer said, "Augustus Washington became a casualty of the change in public sentiment," when at twelve years old he was turned away from the schools that had previously welcomed him. Undaunted, Washington improved his education independently by reading William Lloyd Garrison's weekly newspaper the *Liberator* and Benjamin Lundy's *Genius of Universal Emancipation*, which instilled in him a desire to "become a scholar, a teacher and a useful man." Later, Washington studied briefly at Dartmouth College and eventually settled in Brooklyn, New York, where he took charge of the African Public School.

Throughout his life, Washington was politically active and worked to secure unrestricted voting rights for black citizens in New York. One of his most notable portraits is of abolitionist John Brown.

Of all the mid-nineteenth-century black photographers, **Henry Shepherd** of St. Paul, Minnesota, was the most popular and successful. During his first year in operation in 1887, he earned $7,500, no paltry sum for any businessman, especially a black man. He liked to advertise that his patrons were among all classes, "from the millionaires to day wage workers." Shepherd was among the first African-American photographers to belong to the all-white National Photographers Association of America, and was further honored when his photographs of Tuskegee Institute, a historically black college in Tuskegee, Alabama, were exhibited at the 1900 Paris Exposition.

Brothers **Glenalvin, Wallace, and William Goodridge** began their photographic careers in York, Pennsylvania, in the late 1840s. Glenalvin won a prize for "best ambrotypes" (a cheap tintype photograph) at a York Country Fair in 1863. The brothers moved to Saginaw, Michigan, after the outbreak of the Civil War and reopened their studio there, which the family operated for fifty years. In 1884 the Goodridge brothers were commissioned by the Department of Forestry to photograph images of daily life and work in the Saginaw Valley woodlands.

In the early 1900s, **James Augustus Van Der Zee** (1886–1983) took photography in the black community to new heights. Van Der Zee grew up in a privileged world, and was exposed to music and art very early in life. His parents, who had been servants of President Ulysses Grant, settled in Lenox, Massachusetts, a summer haven for New England's wealthy. The family was one of about six black families there.

Van Der Zee got his first camera when he was in the fifth grade, and took numerous photographs of his family and other people in the community that he developed himself. By the time he was fourteen, Van Der Zee was working

Marcus Garvey in Regalia *by James Augustus Van Der Zee. 1924.*
*Donna Mussenden Van Der Zee, New York City.*

as a darkroom assistant in a concession stand at Gertz Department Store. Despite the fact that he was proficient at using the equipment and popular with the customers, his employer refused to increase his pay. Disheartened, Van Der Zee left the company but shortly after moved to Harlem and opened his own studio. Soon Van Der Zee was photographing Harlem Renaissance celebrities such as writers Langston Hughes and Countee Cullen, musician Duke Ellington, political activist and religious leader Father Devine, and singers Florence Mills and Mamie Smith. But perhaps he is most noted for his photographs of Marcus Garvey, founder of the Universal Negro Improvement Association, a movement that championed racial pride and urged large-scale emigration of blacks to Africa.

Van Der Zee took his art seriously, commenting that he didn't "'take' pictures; he 'made' pictures." His photographs show that sincere, caring attitude. He went to extra lengths to make his subjects look as beautiful and as handsome as possible, often retouching the negatives to eliminate any imperfections in the skin, teeth, and eyes. He used elaborate props in his studio: "posing" chairs, pianos, stuffed animals, gates, and columns. He took great pride in matching the set with the person's personality, and was careful to show his subjects doing something rather than sitting stiffly.

Van Der Zee's business suffered when the Instamatic and Polaroid cameras came out in the 1950s, but was revived in the early 1980s when he photographed great entertainers such as Bill Cosby, Lou Rawls, Muhammad Ali, and Ruby and Ossie Davis. In 1978, Van Der Zee was presented the Living Legacy Award by President Jimmy Carter at the White House and the First Annual Pierre Touisaint Award by Cardinal Cooke at St. Patrick's Cathedral.

In an article on black photographers in *The International Review of African American Art*, photographer and writer Deborah Willis stated that "Gordon Parks is crazy!" That is the way many people perceived **Gordon Parks** (1912– ) during his early years as a photographer, for he was a risk taker who believed he could do anything he dreamed he could do. Actually, the restless, ambitious Parks could do just about anything—write poetry, books, and music; direct movies; and take photographs—and proved all the critics wrong for thinking he couldn't.

Parks was first a photojournalist, a photographer who uses photography to tell a story. He shot some of the most celebrated and provocative photographs in America's history and was the first African-American photographer for *Life* magazine.

Parks's photographic career began while he was working as a waiter on the Northern Pacific Railroad route between Minneapolis, Minnesota, and Seattle, Washington. Often, Parks visited museums in the cities in which the train stopped. One day he came across a magazine with photographs of "down and out" migrant workers published by the Farm Services Administration (FSA), a government agency set up to assist poor farmers during the Dust Bowl years and the Great Depression. Parks could not forget these images. When he reached Seattle, he purchased a camera for $7.50 in a pawnshop, and began taking his own pictures. The manager of an Eastman Kodak store in St. Paul was so impressed with Parks's first photographs that he arranged for an exhibition of his works in downtown Minneapolis in the Eastman Kodak store window.

At the urging of fellow black photographer Charles White, Parks applied for and was awarded a fellowship offered by the Rosenwald Foundation. Later he went to work for the FSA. Roy Emerson Stryker was head of a special photography section of the FSA from 1935 to 1942. Stryker advised Parks to use his camera to subtly express what he saw in segregated Washington, D.C. But Parks felt a rage over racism that could not be expressed subtly. One photograph from this angry period in his professional life was *American Gothic*, which showed what the American dream really meant to black people in the 1940s. The photograph of a cleaning woman, Ella Watson, standing in front of the American flag with a broom in one hand and a mop in the other is an American classic.

Twins **Morgan and Marvin Smith** also documented life in Harlem in the 1930s and 1940s. Through the lenses of their cameras, we can relive the breadlines and political rallies of the Depression, and we can witness the enjoyment Lindy Hoppers were having during the latest dance craze.
Photojournalism became more popular among black photographers during the 1950s and 1960s as the civil rights movement gained momentum. They

American Gothic *by Gordon Parks. 1942. Collections of the Library of Congress, Washington, D.C.*

began to document the movement and the mood of black people for predominately black newspapers and magazines such as *Ebony*, *Jet*, *Sepia*, and *Our World*. By this time, too, colleges and universities offered photography as a part of the schools of journalism, thus producing more professional photojournalists. Whether trained or untrained, African-American photographers had a knack for catching the immediacy of the situation.

# SEVEN

## TO RESTORE AND REVEAL A LEGACY

In the decade following the Civil War (1865–1875), twenty-four historically black colleges were established. Supported by the Freedmen's Bureau, churches, and blacks themselves, these black colleges, or institutes or normal schools as they were called then, flourished. By the 1880s the number of black institutions of higher learning had grown significantly. Today there are roughly 106 historically black colleges and universities.

These black institutions operated on the philosophy of training the "heart, head, and hand," meaning they took into account the education of the "whole" person. Black colleges sought to educate the heart by exposing students to literature, music, and different cultures, and produced some of the most prominent black artists, musicians, and writers in America. Students in historically black colleges were also given a steady diet of Latin, mathematics, the sciences, and the classics, which enabled them to become successful doctors, lawyers, teachers, and other professionals. Training the hand was the doctrine fostered by educators such as Booker T. Washington, founder of Tuskegee Institute, who believed that young people should be taught trades. Therefore, black colleges taught courses in domestic sciences, carpentry, masonry, and nursing to ensure employment after graduation.

The mission of these black colleges to educate the whole person paid off in other ways over the years. They have produced some of the brightest stars in the constellation of twentieth-century musicians, literary personalities, and artists. Aaron Douglas, Hale Woodruff, Elizabeth Catlett, and Archibald Motley are but a few of the stars who benefited from attending or working at a black college.

It is not surprising, then, that these black colleges also became the centers for the study, collection, and conservation of African and African-American art. Thanks to the vision of college founders, art professors, art historians, curators, preservationists, and artists themselves, at least six of the 106 black colleges currently house some of the finest African-American art

*Political Prisoner (cedar with polychrome) by Elizabeth Catlett. 1971. Schomburg Center, New York City.*

in America. These six institutions—Clark University in Atlanta, Georgia; Fisk University in Nashville, Tennessee; Hampton University in Hampton, Virginia; Howard University in Washington, D.C.; North Carolina Central University in Durham, North Carolina; and Tuskegee University in Tuskegee, Alabama—were pioneers in promoting African-American art.

## COLLECTING AFRICAN-AMERICAN ART

For the most part, black colleges began collecting African and African-American art before they had galleries or museums in which to display them. From the very beginning, Hampton University (founded in 1868) emphasized the importance of an art museum and was the first historically black col-

*The Fisk Memorial Chapel, Nashville, Tennessee.*

lege to assemble and house an art collection that was open to everyone regardless of race. Hampton founder General Samuel Chapman Armstrong's fascination with African and Native-American cultures prompted him to collect artifacts from both cultures. By the 1870s an African studies course was offered at Hampton, and the college purchased its first pieces of African art.

Armstrong, like most leaders at historically black colleges, believed in the hands-on method of teaching and learning, so it was important to have artifacts and specimens for students to examine. Until the opening of the art gallery at Howard University in Washington, D.C., in 1928, Hampton University had bragging rights as the storehouse of the largest collection of African, African-American, and Native-American art in the country.

*Frances Benjamin Johnston, "Studying the Butterfly."*
*Hampton University, Hampton, Virginia.*

Collecting the works of nineteenth-century artists such as Henry O. Tanner and others was the first step toward conserving the legacy of the giants in African-American art. However, struggling black colleges did not have the funds to install climate control or to store art in acid-free paper to protect the works they had collected. Neither did they have the finances to hire teachers to teach conservation techniques. Besides, conservation of art was a low priority budgetary item. Thus, over the years many pieces of art deteriorated.

The decade of the 1990s saw a revolution in the collection and preservation of black art. Two men: Richard Powell, chair of the Department of Art and Art History at Duke University in North Carolina, and Jock Reynolds, director of the Yale University art gallery, were at the forefront of conserving black art at black colleges.

Jock Reynolds found his calling while researching African-American art at historically black colleges. "I saw major works by Romare Bearden, Wifredo Lam, Edmonia Lewis, William H. Johnson, and others stacked cheek to jowl," Reynolds told the *Smithsonian Magazine*. The condition of art at the black colleges was heart wrenching; many paintings were punctured and torn.

Reynolds was moved to do something to help. Calling on the expertise of his friend Richard Powell, he developed a restoration plan. Soon the two men called together a group of art conservationists, curators, acclaimed artists, private collectors, and art educators to help restore the deteriorating artistic legacy. Eventually partnerships with universities, businesses, foundations, and art museums were formed. The training of minority students interested in art conservation as a career, through a mentorship program, became a strong component of the committee's mission. Introduced by conservators Joyce Stoner, Leslie Guy, and Ted Stanley, the idea was to interest art students while they were still undergraduates. Their idea led to summer internships, supervised by museum staffs at the Studio Museum of Harlem in New York and the Addison Gallery in Andover, Massachusetts.

"It was incredible," exclaimed one student during an appearance on CBS's *Sunday Morning*. "Because I got a chance to see artwork that I would

*Jock Reynolds and participants at Williamstown Art Conservation Center in Williamstown, Massachusetts.*

see in art history books and [it] gave me a chance to really analyze the technique and brushstrokes and those types of things."

After five years, a project "To Conserve a Legacy" at the Willamstown Art Conservation Center in Massachusetts had trained numerous other African-American art students, who are now filling the dwindling pool of art conservationists at historically black colleges and universities. Under the careful instruction of curators and preservationists, students have restored and preserved 1,400 works. "This is really about conserving not just a physical legacy, but a cultural legacy, a psychological legacy, a mental legacy of perseverance—of creativity," Richard Powell told the host of CBS's *Sunday Morning.*

## PRIVATE COLLECTORS

Black colleges and universities are not the only conservers of black art. Many individuals, too, value black art and are collecting it. Bill and Camille Cosby are serious collectors of African-American art. They paid $250,000 for Henry

O. Tanner's *The Thankful Poor*, the highest price ever paid for a work of art by an African-American artist.

Dr. Lindley Smith, an ophthalmologist in Richmond, Virginia, is another collector of African-American art and currently serves as president of the Friends of African-American Art at the Virginia Museum of Fine Arts. While not as extensive as the collection of the Cosbys, Smith's collection is accessible to ordinary people, mostly African Americans, for he displays it in his office.

Artist and collector David Driskell has amassed over 450 major works of art by such greats as Romare Bearden, Elizabeth Catlett, Lois Mailou Jones, Jacob Lawrence, and Augusta Savage. In his Victorian-style home outside of Washington, D.C., the walls and tables are adorned with beautiful and historic pieces of art. Nature is also beautifully framed by the living room windows—a vista of a large yard and garden that features Driskell's famous bottle tree. (Trees decorated with an assortment of colored glass bottles is a black folk art form that is seen in the rural South.)

Driskell's collection has been documented in a traveling exhibit titled "Narratives of African American Art and Identity," and is one of the best examples of the expression of black heritage and tradition.

Few collectors got in on the ground floor of collecting folk art like Dr. Regenia A. Perry of Richmond, Virginia. Since 1970 she has collected the art of self-taught artists and has collected and installed exhibits of folk art forms made exclusively by black Americans. In 1982 she mounted an exhibition of two hundred pieces from her personal collection at the Anderson Gallery at Virginia Commonwealth University. She called her exhibit "What It Is: Black American Folk Art from the Collection of Regenia Perry."

Together, the conservationists at black colleges and universities, students, the staff at the Willamstown Art Conservation Center, the Studio Museum of Harlem, and individual collectors are conserving the legacy of African-American art and artists.

# GLOSSARY

**Academic style**  A style of art created according to established, traditional ways; containing a formal academic quality.

**Action painting**  An action-packed style; alive with movement.

**Cubism**  An abstract style of art characterized by a flat, two-dimensional surface, lack of perspective, and natural forms fragmented into geometric shapes.

**Expressionism**  An art movement and style that began in Germany in which the artist depicts subjective responses to objects and events.

**Folk art**  Art that is created by people with little or no formal training in art and who work outside the accepted traditions.

**Hudson River School**  A group of mid-nineteenth century landscape painters whose works often incorporated moral and literary themes.

**Impressionism**  An art movement and style that began in France during the 1860s. Impressionists tried to depict the natural appearance of a subject by using dabs or strokes of primary unmixed colors in order to simulate actual reflected light.

**Naive**  A style of painting identified by its simplicity, lack of perspective, and bright colors; unaffected simplicity.

**Primitivism**  The style of art of primitive people or primitive artists. Early, undeveloped, or simple art forms; elemental.

**Romanticism**  An art movement and style popular during the early nineteenth century that emphasized passion over reason and imagination and intuition over logic. Romanticism favors a free expression of the emotions and unrestrained action to show nature in its dramatic, untamed state.

# FURTHER READING

Ashabranner, Brent. *The New African Americans*. North Haven, CT: Shoestring Press, 1999.

Bearden, Romare, and Henderson, Harry. *The History of African-American Artists from 1792 to Present*. New York: Pantheon Books, 1993.

Britton, Crystal A. *African American Art: The Long Struggle*. New York: Smithmark Publishers, 1996.

Butler, Jerry. *A Drawing in the Sand: The Story of African American Art*. New York: Zino Press Children's Books, 1998.

CBS News: *Sunday Morning*, "To Preserve and Protect," May 23, 1999. (Interviews)

Chase, Judith Wragg. *Afro-American Art and Craft*. New York: Van Nostrand Reinhold Company, 1971.

Dover, Cedric. *American Negro Art*. New York: New York Graphic Society, 1960.

Driskell, David C. *Two Centuries of Black American Art*. New York: Knopf, 1976.

Farris, Phoebe, ed. *Women Artists of Color: A Bio-Critical Sourcebook of 20th Century Artists in the Americas*. Westport, CT: Greenwood Press, 1999.

Fry, Gladys-Marie. *Stitched from the Soul: Slave Quilts from the Ante-Bellum South*. New York: Museum of American Folk Art, 1990 (Dutton Studio Books).

Koverman, Jill Beute. *"I made this jar ... Dave": The Life and Works of the Enslaved African-American Potter, Dave*. Columbia, South Carolina: University of South Carolina McKissick Museum, 1998.

Kraskin, Sandra, et al. *Wrestling with History: A Celebration of African American Self-Taught Artists from the Collection of Ronald and June Shelp.* New York: Sidney Mishkin Gallery, Baruch College, City University of New York. 1996.

Lewis, Samella. *African American Art and Artists.* Berkeley: University of California Press, 1990.

———. *Art: African American.* New York: Harcourt Brace Jovanovich, Inc., 1978.

Lyons, Mary E. *Deep Blues: Bill Taylor, Self-Taught Artist.* New York: Houghton Mifflin Company, 1994.

———. *Master of Mahogany: Tom Day, Free Black Cabinetmaker.* New York: Houghton Mifflin Company, 1994.

———. *Starting Home: The Story of Horace Pippin, Painter.* New York: Houghton Mifflin Company, 1993.

———. *Stitching Stars: The Story Quilts of Harriet Powers.* New York: Houghton Mifflin Company, 1993.

———. *Talking With Tebe: Clementine Hunter, Memory Artist.* New York: Houghton Mifflin Company, 1998.

Newton, James E., and Roland L. Lewis. *The Other Slaves: Mechanics, Artisans and Craftsmen.* Boston: G.K. Hall & Company, 1978.

Perry, Regenia A., et al. *Free Within Ourselves: African-American Artists in the Collection of the National Museum of American Art.* Hartford: Wadsworth Atheneum, 1992. (Organized by the National Museum of American Art, Smithsonian Institution, Washington, DC. Published in association with Pomegranate Artbooks, Petaluma.)

———. *Harriet Powers, Bible Quilts.* New York: St. Martin's Press, n.d. (Rizzoli Art Series).

———. *What It Is: Black American Folk Art from the Collection of Regenia Perry*, October 6–27, 1982, Anderson Gallery, Virginia Commonwealth University. (Exhibition catalog)

Porter, James A. *Modern Negro Art.* New York: The Dryden Press, 1943.

Powell, Richard, and Reynolds, Jock. *To Conserve a Legacy: American Art from Historically Black Colleges and Universities.* Boston: MIT Press, 1999.

Riggs, Thomas, ed. *St. James Guide to Black Artists.* Detroit: St. James Press (Gale), 1997.

Skipwith, Joanna. *Rhapsodies in Black: Art of the Harlem Renaissance.* Berkeley, CA: Hayward Gallery, Institute of Visual Arts and the University of California Press, 1997.

Smithsonian Institution, National Museum of American Art. *African-American Art: 19th and 20th-Century Selections.* Washington, DC, n.d. (Exhibition booklet)

Virginia Museum of Fine Arts. *African Art.* Richmond: VMFA, 1994. (Exhibition catalog)

Vlach, John M. *By the Work of Their Hands: Studies in Afro-American Folklife.* Charlottesville: University of Virginia Press, 1991.

Wardlaw, Alvia. *Black Art, Ancestral Legacy: The African Impulse in African-American Art.* Dallas: Dallas Museum of Art, 1989. (Distributed by Harry N. Abrams, Inc., New York.)

Willis, Deborah. *Reflections in Black: A History of Black Photographers 1840 to the Present.* New York: W. W. Norton, 2000.

# INDEX